Low Fee Vegan Investing

Taking veganism to the next level

Tom Nowak, CFP®

Low Fee Vegan Investing

Taking veganism to the next level

Copyright © 2014 Tom Nowak

First Printing

Printed in the United States of America

ISBN-10:   1492802972

ISBN-13:   978-1492802976

DEDICATION

To all who educate others to the many personal, societal and planetary benefits of a vegan diet. The efforts of Colin T. Campbell, PhD; John McDougall, MD; Caldwell Esselstyn, Jr., MD; and Richard Oppenlander, DDS are particularly noted, as their efforts have inspired me to develop a low fee approach to investing for vegans.

CONTENTS

ACKNOWLEDGEMENTS

My sincere thanks to all who helped with their reviews, comments and support, including: Paula Birmingham, Catherine Hawley, Kathy Hankard, Julie Nowak, Mary Harris-King of CS2, Owen Moore (cover art), Richard Gussow, Amy Dickinson and Abby Morton. Collectively, you have helped me transform a concept into a readable guide for vegans, vegetarians and even meatless-Monday investors.

INTRODUCTION

In March of 2012, my first book, *Low Fee Socially Responsible Investing; Investing in your worldview on your terms*, provided the details of an investment approach that could be used by investors and their advisors to construct a small portfolio of stocks that was in alignment with a particular worldview.[1] One limitation of this methodology is that it is primarily applicable to views easily defined by a set of negative and positive screens. More intricate worldviews could not be accommodated. Also, the book only addressed socially responsible equity investments. It did not discuss fixed income investments which are used to better manage the overall risk level of a portfolio. In order to address these deficiencies and expand upon my experience in this area over the past two years, this book addresses the question "What approach could a vegan use?" That is, what screening – positive or negative – is applicable for someone with a vegan worldview?

During the past several years, I have developed a number of portfolios that reflect a wide range of topics of interest to socially responsible investors. For the most part, these portfolios were developed with the aid of published data which rank large publicly held companies on parameters such as political accountability, type of industry (e.g. fossil fuel), use of green technology, faith-based values, etc. The effort to date has met my expectations in illustrating the benefits of low fee passive investing, applied to the area of socially responsible investing.

For those unfamiliar with socially responsible investing (SRI), picture a large grouping of stocks that might be in a typical mutual fund designed to represent a snapshot of the economy and provide investment returns that might be expected for such a diversified mixture (e.g. a benchmark index fund). In SRI investing, the first step is to define the universe of stocks that make it through the first filter (e.g. top 500 of the largest US-based companies). The next step would be to exclude (a negative screen) companies that are in industries which are not attractive to a given class of investors (e.g. tobacco, alcohol or gun manufacturers). Where appropriate, a set of positive attributes or screens are then used to further define the portfolio (e.g. best 100 company list for a desired behavior, relatively good rating in disclosure of political contributions, etc.). The final cut might be to screen for financial stability ratings, especially in the case where active portfolio management or market timing is not an objective. In passive portfolio management, the investment mix might typically be reviewed only once per year.

During the course of writing the first book, coincidentally (I think), I made a change in my eating habits. Instead of maintaining a "semi-vegetarian" diet, I was compelled to try a vegan diet after reading *The China Study*[2] and being asked by my doctor to start taking a statin drug to reduce a cholesterol level that was stubbornly moving above the current guideline. Having a background as a scientist in a pharmaceutical company, I knew that statin drugs, popular as they are, were not magic bullets. Also, I did not see I had that much to lose. What is now a very familiar story to vegans, in a matter of months my cholesterol level lowered considerably and my blood pressure and weight dropped as well, simply by making plant-based substitutions for meat and dairy products in my diet.

After doing more research on the topic of veganism and watching a number of relevant documentaries, a vegan worldview gradually materialized (in my mind, at least). After examining a fair number of vegan issues from an investment screening perspective, I wanted to be in a position to offer a vegan-screened portfolio to anyone who might be interested, just as I was. Unfortunately, however, I could not find established vegan mutual funds or other financial instruments to use as a hint of what companies vegans would invest in, given the chance. There appeared to be no published rankings of how large companies ranked in terms of their appeal to vegans. When the concept first struck me, it appeared as if it would be futile to develop a set of parameters that could be used to define a vegan worldview. With the passion of a convert, however, I could not let the idea rest. This book presents the results of that effort.

A primary motivation in developing a low fee approach to vegan investing is my belief that vegans are prime candidates for appreciating and utilizing the benefits of sustainable and responsible (SR) investing. Eating a plant-based diet, at least historically, has required a personal investment of time and commitment. With the increased availability of meat and dairy substitutes in both ingredients and ready-to-cook options, the amount of additional meal preparation time investment appears to be steadily diminishing, but is still present. The simple act of identifying a vegan-friendly restaurant when dining out shows a willingness to make an extra effort. In addition to the demonstrated commitment to individual health, the commitment to societal and planetary health is often a core motivation that is shared by many SR investors.

Another motivation in writing this book is that a movement to a plant-based diet significantly reduces an individual's environmental footprint (less energy use, less water use, less disease). Vegan investing can be a tool for vegans and non-vegans to further contribute to a more sustainable world.

It is easy to dismiss the idea of sustainable and responsible or vegan investing as there are many myths and obstacles to overcome. First, a majority of financial advisors and intermediaries are not familiar enough with the area to be in a position to provide assistance or advice. Second, inertia favors inaction rather than action; a convenient myth can be used to put the idea aside (e.g. it is too hard to identify an appropriate investment mix, investment performance may suffer, investment expenses are too high, etc.). For many investors, concern over hypocrisy is a factor. For instance, if I divest my portfolio from fossil fuel companies, I need to reconcile my current fossil fuel footprint in all aspects of my lifestyle and clearly identify my position (e.g. fossil fuel divestment does not equal an immediate cessation of fossil fuel usage, but does reduce factors that hinder development of better alternatives). It is my belief that most vegans more readily come to grips with a world where all is not black and white. For instance, a person who adopts a vegan diet, when challenged with a question regarding his existing car's leather seats (or her leather purse), does not throw his or her hands up in the air, give up and order a cheeseburger for lunch. Relatively better food and consumption choices are considered an *improvement* to most vegans. The occasional deviation does not invalidate the larger gains. Degrees of hypocrisy are dealt with, out of necessity. Criticisms are understood for what they often are – ignorance, rationalization, self-validation, or mental laziness on the part of the critic.

Disclaimer

This book contains guidance on how to build a customized portfolio that reflects a vegan worldview with a minimum of professional assistance, and can be implemented and maintained inexpensively. You should treat the contents of this book as you would a sharp knife: if used carefully, you may be able to cut your investment costs substantially and produce satisfying results. If you are an inexperienced investor and use this book without at least a few hours of professional guidance, you may hurt yourself financially. We all have unique financial circumstances and prior investment knowledge. The suggestions in this book are not to be treated as specific investment, tax or legal advice.

Any references to investment performance are historical in nature. Past performance does not guarantee future results, and all investments entail risk of loss, including the potential for loss of principal. Each investor is unique, and factors including his or her investment experience, tax situation, time horizon, tolerance for risk and fluctuations in value should be weighed carefully before making an investment decision. Mutual funds are sold by prospectus only, and the investor should carefully review the current prospectus for any fund considered before investing.

The views expressed in this book are solely those of the author and do not necessarily represent the views of any organization that the author is associated with. The author does not receive any fees for mention of any source of information or service provider. The data and calculations represent the author's best effort to be fair and accurate, however no guarantee is made.

CHAPTER 1

Low Fee Sustainable and Responsible Investing

Much attention is placed in my first book on defining "low fee" investing. This chapter assumes it has been some time since you read it and would appreciate a refresher or, instead, a brief summary. Also, it may be helpful to discuss the various flavors of socially responsible investing (caution: there may be some food-based terms used throughout the book to spice things up).

If investment fees are not at all an issue, it would not take a lot of research to identify an investment advisor willing and able to develop a portfolio that could be tailored to a specific worldview, veganism included. An advisor, after spending a significant amount of time with an investor, could discuss which companies and which groups of companies (sectors) appeal to and/or repel from the standpoint of the products or services they supply. In order to make the proposition work for the advisor, however, a minimum fee of $5,000, if not $10,000 per year or more, would be typical. To make this practical for an investor, a minimum investment amount of $1,000,000 is required to make the fee seem tolerable (($10,000/$1,000,000) x 100 = 1.0%).

In my first book, I defined "low fee" as a point where both investment management and financial planning is provided at a cost of less than 0.5% per year. In a world where the long-term return of investments appears to be moving lower, it becomes important to keep investment fees as low as practical. Also, many investors are not aware of the fees they currently pay and are not aware that they really cannot afford to lose up to half of the opportunity cost of their nest egg to fees over the course of their investment lives.

An example I have previously used is as follows:

$100,000 grows to $768,609 over 35 years at a 6% annual growth rate. With a 2% per year fee, the same $100,000 grows only 4% annually to $394,610 over the same 35-year period.

When I issued my first book in March of 2012, I was unaware that a new brokerage platform would soon be rolled out later that spring.[3] This new platform, Motif Investing, brought the cost of investing in a specific idea (theme-based investing) down to a new low, $9.95 for a basket of up to 30 stocks, directly owned. With no ongoing management fees, theme-based investing costs took a quantum leap downward. It was not much later when Motif Investing introduced a build-your-own portfolio tool that could further facilitate a low fee approach to socially responsible investing. Other low-cost platforms can work and, in some cases, may provide other features and offerings of interest. For comparison, a 50-stock custom portfolio could be acquired for $ 120 (plus annual $60 low activity fee) using the Folio Investing® platform.[4] Depending upon your specific needs, an attractive fee structure can be identified using other low-cost platforms.

With the availability of custom-built mini-stock portfolios for as low as $9.95 (bare minimum fund management fee), the base price for low-fee impact investing has reached a new level of affordability. For do-it-yourselfers, the advisor fee is zero. An investment portfolio of $2,000 would have an expense ratio equivalent to just under 0.5% ($9.95 * 100/$2,000). An investment portfolio of $10,000 would have an expense ratio equivalent to just under 0.1%, comparable to a low cost index fund. Larger portfolio sizes result in an expense ratio that approaches zero.

For most investors, the use of an hourly, fee-only, advisor is recommended in order to achieve the benefits of low fee impact/vegan investing. An advisor can help with the following:

1) Assure that a proper balance of risk/reward is established (allocation).
2) Assure sufficient diversification (e.g. use of more than one mini-stock portfolio, use of suitable fixed income investments).
3) Address tax planning opportunities (e.g. good use of taxable and tax-advantaged accounts).
4) Take other accounts, such as employer-provided retirement accounts, into consideration in overall portfolio design.
5) Evaluate how other income-producing sources, such as charitable gift annuities, might fit into your financial plan.
6) Provide other ideas on how your worldview can be expressed in your investment mix.

The advisor fee for assistance with vegan investing will depend upon the advisor's established hourly fee (typical range between $150 and $300 per hour) and the advisor's familiarity and access to low cost investment platforms. In instances where an advisor has established investment mixes and does not need to reinvent the wheel on your behalf, the fee for investment advice would consist of the time needed for the advisor to fulfill his fiduciary responsibility to act in your best interest. This would include establishing your risk profile and understanding your investment needs before developing and making specific recommendations. The amount of time is often impacted by the size and complexity of your portfolio. You should expect an advisor to provide you with an anticipated fee range after you both have come to an understanding of the scope of the engagement.

Advisors charging by commission or assets under management are not, in my opinion, generally in a position to provide low fee investment management services to guide vegan investors due to the limitations of their fee models. For an investor with a large vegan investing portfolio, a negotiated fee might lower the expense ratio somewhat. However, the typical minimum I have observed is $10,000 (for a $1,000,000 portfolio this would equate to a 1% expense ratio). Advisors paid by commission typically require that an existing mutual fund is established and that a sales charge can be applied (e.g. A share fund class). To date, I have not identified a vegan-themed mutual fund.

Chapter 2

Defining a Vegan Worldview

I often use the term "socially responsible investing" to represent an assortment of investment approaches. As the history of investing has progressed, a fair number of terms have been introduced to more precisely define the nature and objective of the process. For instance, *faith-based* investing would be used to describe a portfolio screened using the principles of a specific faith/religion. *Green investing*, like *Sustainable Investing*, would tend to apply environmentally-focused criteria of a product, service or company. *Ethical investing* would take corporate governance practices into primary consideration. *Impact investing* intends to generate social and environmental impact. The concept of vegan investing appears to fit comfortably in the general category of sustainable and responsible investing. Of course, there is plenty of overlap with the other categories, depending upon the individual investor's worldview.

One of the most memorable discussions about the consequence of acting on one's worldview, or ideology, occurred during an October 23rd, 2008 PBS broadcast.[5] The following is a partial transcript of a discussion on the housing bubble between Representative Henry Waxman and Alan Greenspan, the former Chairman of the Federal Reserve:

REP. HENRY WAXMAN: The question I have for you is, you had an ideology, you had a belief that free, competitive – and this is your statement – "I do have an ideology. My judgment is that free, competitive markets are by far the unrivaled way to organize economies. We've tried regulation. None meaningfully worked." That was your quote.

You had the authority to prevent irresponsible lending practices that led to the subprime mortgage crisis. You were advised to do so by many others. And now our whole economy is paying its price.

Do you feel that your ideology pushed you to make decisions that you wish you had not made?

ALAN GREENSPAN: Well, remember that what an ideology is, is a conceptual framework with the way people deal with reality. Everyone has one. You have to -- to exist, you need an ideology. The question is whether it is accurate or not.

And what I'm saying to you is, yes, I found a flaw. I don't know how significant or permanent it is, but I've been very distressed by that fact.

REP. HENRY WAXMAN: You found a flaw in the reality...

ALAN GREENSPAN: Flaw in the model that I perceived is the critical functioning structure that defines how the world works, so to speak.

REP. HENRY WAXMAN: In other words, you found that your view of the world, your ideology, was not right, it was not working?

ALAN GREENSPAN: That is – precisely. No, that's precisely the reason I was shocked, because I had been going for 40 years or more with very considerable evidence that it was working exceptionally well.

Although few of us make individual decisions that can significantly impact the world economy, we do make frequent decisions that impact our personal economic well-being and those around us. As noted in the dialog, we all have an ideology or worldview regarding investing – the question, indeed, is whether it is accurate or not.

One of the safe-harbor worldviews regarding investing that has become increasing popular over the last several decades has been to utilize low cost, passively managed index funds. A handful of index funds representing the basic asset classes (domestic and international stocks, government and corporate bonds), balanced to one's risk profile and time horizon, can provide for a simple and effective investment plan. Index funds contain the stocks of a relatively large number of companies that define a segment of the economy - per the worldview of the institution that is charged with defining the composition of the index (e.g. Standard & Poor's 500). Essentially, there is no significant amount of discrimination between companies that are best-in-class or worst-in-class on any measure, except, perhaps, their size (cost it would take to buy all outstanding shares and take the company into private hands) in relation to the total investible market.

Many financial advisors, me included, often recommend the use of index funds. It is simple and has historically resulted in near-benchmark performance based upon the risk level taken (i.e. allocation between stocks and fixed income investments).

There are instances, however, where an investor's worldview cannot be comfortably accommodated with the use of index funds. The increased popularity of sustainable and responsible investing is due to sensitivities of profiting from economic activity that is inconsistent with one's worldview or values. For example, some investors want to avoid holding stocks of companies primarily involved in tobacco, alcohol, firearms, for-profit prisons, and/or fossil fuels, to name a few (i.e., negative screens). Other investors might want to specifically tilt their investment mix into companies with best-of-class behavior in the area of political accountability, employee relations, or sustainable environmental practices (i.e., positive screens).

There are numerous mutual funds available that accommodate many of the negative and positive screens just noted. Also, the portfolio construction approach noted in my first book has been applied to an assortment of value sets where the screening criteria are readily available. In order to develop a portfolio that is consistent with a vegan worldview in a cost-effective manner, it is necessary to define such a worldview in terms of investments that are available.

The subjectivity in identifying good versus bad companies on a given attribute limits the appeal of sustainable and responsible (or vegan) investing for many investors and advisors. In my opinion, this issue is best addressed by using a transparent, clearly-communicated set of criteria and refining these criteria as new information develops. The alternative of indiscriminately holding the stocks of many companies that are inconsistent with one's worldview and values is certainly not any more appealing.

Before delving into defining my assessment of a vegan's worldview from an investment perspective, a huge disclaimer is in order. I am confident that my definitions will not be in perfect – or even good – alignment with the views of a significant percentage of fellow vegans. Ironically, I may even butcher one of your sacred cows along the way. Acceptance of some imperfection, however, is a necessity if progress is to be made. Also, out of regulatory necessity, I am not going to be making specific investment recommendations down to the company level in this book. My intent is that anyone using the information in this book, make the appropriate adjustments and obtain sufficient advice so that her or his worldview is achieved to the extent practical.

Another disclaimer is that I am not taking a position as to the precise definition of vegan (e.g. are you still a vegan if you own any products with animal-sourced components such as a leather belt?). In the area of sustainable and responsible investing, it is very common to have a mixed portfolio. For instance, many 401(k) plan choices do not have a socially responsible fund available, let alone one that is likely to even approximate your worldview. Also, I believe it is very appropriate for investors to choose the ratio between screened and un-screened investments as this allows them to develop a comfort level with a potentially new investment approach. It is analogous to starting with a meatless Monday, then adding an extra day per month as one's pantry, freezer and menu is transitioned.

In my experience, individuals choose to follow a vegan diet for one of the following reasons:

- To improve or maintain good health
- To significantly decrease their carbon footprint
- To avoid unnecessary cruelty to animals
- To adhere to religious or cultural influences

The above four topics are interwoven into economic activity on a personal, national and global scale and, therefore, make it natural to consider them from the standpoint of vegan investing.

As noted in the introduction, my first motivation to choose a vegan diet was the desire for good health without the use of prescription drugs. Upon further study and awareness, it became apparent that all four factors played a role in justifying some additional effort in the area of food choice. One of my goals in writing this book is to demonstrate how investing can support these existing motivations.

No matter how one decides to become a vegan, it has been my experience that most vegans are aware, or are in the process of becoming aware, of all of the benefits of their food choice preference.

One of the arguments against most types of socially responsible investing is that, by definition, diversification suffers when a decision is made to exclude various groups or sectors of stocks that would otherwise be part of a larger investable universe. If diversification is good, then the natural tendency is to have as much of it as possible. Fortunately, this does not have to be a big problem if some safeguards are in place. It is important to recognize that stocks of many of the largest corporations tend to move in lock step with each other. In other words, their performance behaviors are relatively correlated. One example would be to compare the performance history of the Dow 30 and the S&P 500. With only 30 stocks, the Dow and S&P 500 often move in tandem over multi-year time frames. This should not be unexpected since the stocks of the Dow 30 constitute a significant amount of the S&P 500 weighting. Admittedly, 500 stock holdings provide more diversification than 30. Total diversification implies ownership of every publicly-held company in the world, proportional to its share of world economic activity. At some point, due to cost and practicality, a limit is reached.

From my perspective, risk management, rather than diversification, is how an impact or social investor can eliminate the need for overly broad diversification. How many holdings are needed to manage risk? This can be determined by your needs and objectives. For instance, how many companies did Warren Buffett have in his $105.8 billion dollar Berkshire Hathaway portfolio as of March 31, 2014? – 45.[6]

John Maynard Keynes, the legendary economist who had a significant influence on a number of notable figures in the investment world was not excessively diversified (e.g. 1934 P.R. Finance U.S. Stock Holdings lists stocks of 22 companies).[7,8] He tended to use a worldview approach as did the more modern investment guru Peter Lynch.[9] I am not saying that index investing is not a valid or often preferable approach to investing – just that it is limited in the sense that it requires you to own, support and benefit from economic activities you may find absolutely repulsive.

Vegan stereotypes

On the one hand, it is very inappropriate to stereotype any group. Clearly there is a considerable amount of diversity among vegans: Was someone born into a vegan family? Is one the lone wolf vegan in a family? On the other hand, an attempt to identify some common characteristics is essential if a vegan portfolio or investing philosophy is to be attempted.

It has been my experience that vegans tend to be very aware of how their food choices contribute to, or in some cases, challenge their health. If health was a primary motivator for adopting a vegan diet, then one is especially familiar with the health benefits.

Although it is possible to be an obese vegan, I have not often observed this (it would require a significant dietary tilt towards fatty plant-based oils or a lot of empty sugar calories provided by choices such as soft drinks). For converts, the adoption of more exercise into their lifestyle tends to correlate with the dietary change and a relatively improved level of fitness is often evident.

It is easy to be dismissive of the health claims or the reports by various well-known celebrity converts of the health benefits. The news is saturated with get-fit-quick schemes and skepticism is understandable. Health-motivated vegans will be quick to recommend many of the books published by well-respected sources such as Drs. Campbell, McDougall, and Esselstyn, so that an independent investigation can be made.[10,11,12]

With the increased awareness of global climate change and the impact of food choice on the accumulation of greenhouse gases (GHG), another group of vegans is likely to grow: environmentally motivated vegans. Authors such as Dr. Oppenlander and others lay out a clear case for how food choice has been a very significant contributor to the increase of global greenhouse gas emissions. His book, *Food Choice and Sustainability*, contains a wealth of information.[13] A brief summary of some of the key points in this book are provided here to illustrate the sensitivities of environmentally aware vegans:

- "The single largest component of agricultural emissions are those from raising livestock, which contributes, at a minimum, between 18 percent and 51 percent of all total GHG emissions globally."
- "Agriculture occupies 55 percent of the land in the contiguous United States but livestock and the crops grown to feed them occupy 78 percent of that agricultural land."
- "While we use less than 1 percent of all water consumed for drinking purposes in the U.S. –

50 percent of all the water used in the U.S. is given to the animals we eat."

- "It takes over 5,000 gallons of water to produce 1 pound of meat"

For many vegans, whether religious-based or not, the avoidance of meat and dairy products is simply a matter of a respect for animals. As the need for productive food processing has increased to serve an ever-expanding global population, it has become clear that productivity gains have often been made at the expense of increased cruelty to animals.[14,15]

Religious belief as well as cultural influences can compel dietary choice (see Chapter 12).

I have observed that most vegans have a significant awareness of all of the various benefits and rationales that support their food choice. It is this awareness that makes it apparent to me that many of the typical filters used in socially responsible investing would be of interest to a vegan. Where the term "green investing" might be a conversation stopper in some circles, this is not a topic that instantly repels vegans. I find that vegans acquire a healthy skepticism of new ideas (e.g. latest fad diet), yet are open minded and have an inquisitive nature.

Vegans are ahead of the curve. A good analogy might be how attitudes towards cigarette smoking have evolved over the years. First a cool thing to do; then something deemed as not healthy; next something barred from public places and a constant source of additional taxes in order to make sure smokers and tobacco companies pay for the true cost of this activity ("More than $289 billion a year, including at least $133 billion in direct medical care for adults and more than $156 billion in lost productivity" according to a 2014 report by the Surgeon General).[16] The meat and dairy industries have, following the example of the tobacco industry, done an effective job of making consumption of unsustainable and unhealthy levels of their products "cool." Attacks against early signs of increased taxes on unhealthy behavior (infamous New York City soda tax), are following a familiar glide path. Vegans know where this is leading – they have the first-hand information and perspective. They see a day when meat and dairy users will no longer be in the majority as the true cost of this behavior is incorporated into the price and perception of the products.

Equating meat and dairy consumption to smoking is not likely to be generally acceptable for some time. However, many of folks reading this may remember when cigarette smoking was viewed as glamorous. Once society realized the cost of this behavior in terms of human suffering and financial capital, movement toward restricting the practice and minimizing externalized cost eventually took shape.

Fossil fuel consumption is a current example that has a similar dynamic to both tobacco use and food choice. For many years, the fossil fuel industry was allowed to provide a product without any consideration of the cost that future generations would pay as a result of the carbon dioxide released into the atmosphere. Although the realization has been slow, it is now apparent that several fossil fuel providers are including a carbon tax of some sort in their business plans. Groups such as Citizens' Climate Lobby are working diligently to encourage legislation that will put a price on carbon and provide a predictable mechanism to establish a price that will significantly reduce greenhouse gas emissions.[17]

The art and science of long-term investing rewards those who look without bias towards future opportunities, risks and rewards. Who wants to invest in companies that are dependent upon heavy subsidies in an era where public pressure may make it increasingly difficult to hide the true costs associated with poor policies?

Chapter 3

Screening Stocks

As previously noted, individual companies will not be mentioned for several reasons. Since I am an investment advisor, this could be viewed as providing specific advice without a service agreement or knowledge of an individual reader's situation and needs. Second, whether an individual company screens in or out may change over the course of time.

A successful example of a divestment campaign is the one used during the anti-apartheid movement in South Africa. The current fossil fuel divestment campaign appears to be gaining momentum as of the summer of 2014.[18] Both of these movements are examples of how the actions of investors can influence social policy. In my view, vegans also have an opportunity to influence social behavior and policy if they selectively invest only in companies that are compatible with their world view.

As previously noted, index investing is popular, effective and typically a low-cost approach to investing. [19] For the last several decades, index funds have been available and present the opportunity to obtain, essentially, benchmark performance. I would suspect many golfers would like the idea of achieving par performance outing after outing – especially if their primary goal was to enjoy the weather, the companionship, and get a little exercise. Financial planners sometimes note to their clients that shooting par is all they need in order to meet their financial goals. They do not have to tear the cover off of the ball and risk finding themselves in the rough.

For a person who is pretty sure or fearful that they have a wrong-headed view of the world, it is a relatively safer idea to be an index investor – simply own a little bit of most of the investable universe in a proportion that appears to define the world economy to the folks that decide such things. Alternatively, if you believe you have a reasonable world view, but have no need or desire to express this through your financial capital, then why not stick with index investing?

If you are a vegan, I suspect you might want to align your financial capital with the values you live with each meal or even each purchase. If this is the case, and you are in a financial position to have some of your money in the stock market, then there is some work to do. First, define an initial universe of potential stocks to invest in (positive screen). Next, decide what to toss out (negative screen). Finally, establish a discipline that might contribute to a satisfactory outcome.

Large Company Holdings

One of the most popular benchmarks when investing in stocks is the Standard & Poor's 500 (S&P 500 for short). As the number implies, there are 500 relatively large companies owned by common stock holders in this group.

For the initial positive screen, the S&P 500 could be used as a starting point in defining the initial universe. For vegan investors who identify with many of the traditional screens used in sustainable and responsible investing, the initial positive screen could include one or more of the broad groups of stocks in this subset (i.e. most common bad-actor products and services already screened out, most common positive environmental or governance parameters screened in).

To facilitate discussion of the next level of screening (what to toss out), it is helpful to look at 10 of the most identifiable sectors of the investable universe (e.g. information technology, financials, health care...). In some cases, entire sectors might be excluded, thereby simplifying the mechanics of building a suitable portfolio.

Information Technology (IT)

In general, this is a promising area for a vegan investor. IT firms may serve hamburgers in their cafeterias but that is not their core business. More information building and sharing favors the vegan agenda – i.e. spreading the benefits of a vegan lifestyle. Increasing the number of vegans, or those tilting vegan in their diet, provide for more food choices and convenience. It is helpful that this sector of the economy is currently one of the largest by capitalization (i.e. the price it would take to own all of the shares of all of the companies in the sector). Having a large number of companies to choose from allows for further screening to occur while still providing for a workable level of diversification.

Financials

Like the IT sector, most banks, brokerage firms and insurance companies do not manufacture meat or dairy products. Upon closer examination, however, I would tend to recommend against use of this sector in a low fee vegan portfolio. Most of the financial sector does not thrive in, or support, a low fee world of financial services. As investors become empowered throughout the world, I believe there will be a tendency to put more pressure on fees. It is hard for me to imagine that the upcoming generation of social-media savvy investors will hand over significant fees to the financial services industry and maintain the lack of awareness of their parents' generation as to the amount of lost opportunity. Recent times have demonstrated that while this area is profitable for the companies, the headline risk of this sector may be too high for a conservative passive investor. Until it is clear that this sector has fully recovered from the consequences of the subprime mortgage crisis (2007-2009), it would seem appropriate to proceed with caution.

Also, the prospects for casualty insurance companies in the era of climate change possess much uncertainty. As a result of carbon dioxide at levels never seen before in human history, the historical data used to set premiums may no longer be adequate.[20]

Health Care

Baby boom demographics certainly favor the consumption of more health care for years to come. Also, next to food and clean air, health care is a high priority. Whether by education or cost-induced motivation, a global movement towards a vegan diet will reduce the demand for many existing health care products and services that contribute to the economic activity in this sector. The work of many of prominent medical professionals make it clear that diseases of affluence (cancer, heart disease, obesity…) exist primarily due to poor food choices and that they can be prevented and, in many cases, reversed by a vegan diet.[10,11,12] Note that these doctors do not claim that all cases of the diseases of affluence can be treated or prevented - just the majority. For traditional investors, it is primarily about relative growth rates and this sector could be negatively impacted if food choice decisions move steadily in a healthier direction.

Another reason for some vegan investors to avoid this sector is the issue of animal testing. Although the use of animals in testing has diminished from earlier times, it still exists. All considered, this is a sector that could be generally avoided. Depending upon the amount of time and energy one may want to use in the screening process, this sector may still be looked at on a company-by-company basis. Generally, however, a low-fee approach requires a simple, effective and disciplined process in building the portfolio.

Consumer Discretionary

This sector is a mixed bag. Some companies in this sector provide goods and services that would not necessarily, in my opinion, go against the grain. The sector does contain some clearly identifiable food and beverage companies that benefit from nurturing an addiction to a fat, sugar and salt diet. Therefore, the sector should be used with some thoughtfulness.

It may become more practical to invest in this sector if independent ratings measured from a vegan perspective become easily available.

Industrials

This is another mixed bag sector. For the most part, many of these companies make or provide services that do not screen favorably with the basic SRI filters. In general, a vegan world consumes less by living closer to the bottom of the food chain. There may be a few companies in this sector that might be considered.

Energy

In the large company stock area, this is a relatively easy call. A vegan diet requires less energy to produce by an order of magnitude.[13] Traditional energy sectors have identified about 4 times more fossil fuel reserves (carbon) than can be used if we are to have a chance at stabilizing the carbon dioxide concentration of our atmosphere.[21] Many companies in the energy sector are valued based on the presumption that most of the fossil fuel resources under their control will be extracted, developed and sold. These resources can end up being left in the ground (stranded) if taxes, regulations, or sustainable energy alternatives are combined to address the issue of excess green house gases. The issue of stranded assets, alone, might give pause to a long-term investor. This is not to say that vegans do not drive cars or fly in airplanes. The divestment movement, participated in by vegan and non-vegans, is about lowering the barriers to the development and use of alternative energy. The continued subsidy of fossil fuels is not healthy policy. Renewable energy companies, on the other hand, could certainly be candidates for a vegan portfolio, provided that adjustments are made for the additional risks present due to their relatively smaller size and the uncertainties about which alternative technologies and companies will prosper.

Consumer Staples

For the most part, companies in this sector include the tobacco and sugar water providers. In general, this is an easy sector to avoid. Although many of these companies have been historically very profitable, a society that reacts to externalized cost will make it hard for profits to continue to grow.

Materials

Many of the companies that operate in the sector are key players in, if not the definition of, big agriculture. Vegans tend to prefer small to medium agriculture. It is not that vegans do not eat corn or soybeans. The problem is that most of the corn and soybeans produced by big agriculture is used to feed livestock. This extra food chain step uses an unsustainable amount of energy, water and land.[13]

Utilities

In the large company area, this sector is another relatively easy call. Although vegans use electricity and natural gas, the movement towards renewable and decentralized energy production will move ahead faster if investment in the historic players in this area is avoided. The use of renewable energy (e.g. solar and wind) in commercial energy production, however, represents a potential investment opportunity. In time, some of the large companies in this area may convert a significant amount of their operations to renewable energy. At some point, reconsideration could be appropriate.

Telecommunication Services

Although many vegans do not understand their phone or cable bills any better than non-vegans, companies in this area may be appropriate areas of investment. Like information technology, the prospects of more use of communication (simpler, more productive), would appear to be supportive of getting the vegan story more widely communicated. Also, the core business of telecommunications services does not appear to have inherent conflicts for a vegan investor.

Mining

A relatively easy call, I think. The use of precious metals such as gold and silver takes an unnecessary toll on the planet and the humans used to mine them. For more basic ores, there is no compelling case to include this sector in a vegan portfolio. In my opinion, a vegan worldview tries to tilt toward more recycling, less aggressive growth of big infrastructure and centralization. Mining of rare earth elements used in development of sustainable energy solutions (wind, solar, batteries) represents a conundrum – not an area where simple assessments can be applied.

From a practical standpoint, before we start clipping out sectors and stocks, let us look at what we want to accomplish in the way of a finished product. First of all, some folks, not just vegans, think that all, if not most publicly held corporations are just plain bad actors. In some cases, some individuals will be able to avoid this type of investment (stocks of publicly held companies), but this is not a practical solution for most of us. Nor does it need to be if we calibrate our sensitivities – going from an all-of-the-above investment approach to a best-in-class, best-in-my-worldview approach (lesser of the evils).

Another group of investors, vegans included, are fine with most corporate behavior and simply want to position themselves to avoid what could be disproportionate downside risk of having too many companies in their portfolio that will fail miserably if their worldview plays out (e.g., just as buggy whip manufacturers did not do well with the arrival of the automobile, so may fossil fuel companies flounder as alternative energy replaces carbon-based sources).

Most financial advisors typically recommend a stock portfolio that is representative of the larger economy - a mix of very large companies, medium-sized companies and small companies, domestic and non-domestically owned. Besides diversification, one benefit of this approach is that it takes advantage of the stability of larger companies by having a high percentage in this area. Over the long haul, however, small companies provide somewhat more growth than larger companies providing for a risk-balanced approach for many investors.

One of the dilemmas of any variety of green investing (e.g. wind, solar, water technology, vegan), is that there really are not (yet) any very large companies that focus solely in this area. For so-called "pure plays" it is impossible to identify which small companies are likely to be successful in the long term and it is necessary to tread carefully. Fortunately, there are a growing number of companies in this area and it is becoming more practical to develop a diversified mix of holdings on a theme of particular interest.

So what would be an appropriate goal? Based on my experience with other themes (see www.lowfeesociallyresponsibleinvesting.com), I would want to identify between 20 and 30 large company stocks that would be suitable for a passively-managed portfolio (i.e., have financial stability ratings indicating that they are relatively sound). To cover the small and mid-sized area (typically between 0 to 30% of the equity allocation, depending upon the investor's risk profile, time horizon and need for simplicity), it might be helpful to target at least two themes that would be consistent with a vegan worldview. This would result in holding at least 40 to 60 different companies in this area.

If owning a larger collection of stocks is desired, a growing number of SRI funds are screening out fossil fuels. The combination of general SRI criteria (i.e. filter out alcohol, tobacco, firearms, screen in good governance) along with taking out fossil fuels may provide for a satisfactory portfolio mix. Most importantly, the relatively recent establishment of an SRI fossil fuel index by the FTSE Group with BlackRock and the National Resources Defense Council opens up the door to low fee exchange traded funds and, perhaps, mutual funds.

Regarding an investment platform, use of a discount broker that allows for holding partial shares of stock can be an attractive option (e.g., Folio Investing® and Motif Investing allow for partial share ownership and have relatively low fees), especially for investors with limited funds. High-net-worth investors (e.g., typically over $1,000,000 invested) may not need to be as concerned with the need to own partial shares of stock.

Typical Example of Building a Portfolio

To build the portfolio, start with the top 50 to 100 stocks often held in the largest (by asset size) socially responsible funds (active or passive).

Screen out companies based on the sector-by-sector issues discussed.

Screen in the financially more stable companies (i.e., rated in the top 40% based on financial stability or credit rating).

Screen out using any other established criteria of your choosing (it's *your* worldview after all). In establishing criteria, it is helpful if this screen can be applied consistently. This discipline should make future reconstruction and rebalancing simpler.

Review the final stock list subjectively per your worldview. How does this look *versus* the alternative?

Develop back-test data for an equally weighted mix of the top 20 to 30 choices. Advisors typically use commercially available software to do this. It simply involves entering the holdings and the targeted percentages of each stock. The resulting report compares how the portfolio would have performed versus a benchmark collection of holdings over several long time periods (e.g. 3, 5 and 10 years). Individuals may find that the brokerage platform they use has the capability to generate comparable data.

It is recommended that you monitor the forward performance of the portfolio mix prior to investing real dollars. As with back-testing, commercial software of brokerage platform-provided tools may be useful. Familiarity with the volatility of the mix should help reduce anxiety and limit disappointment.

My earlier book, *Low Fee Socially Responsible Investing*, provides more information on how additional factors (i.e., screens) may be used. For a portfolio mix of fewer than 50 stocks, an initial equal allocation helps protect from one bad apple spoiling the overall performance. An equal allocation of a 25-stock portfolio would initially hold 4% of each stock. A market-weighted allocation (i.e., one that takes a company's relative economic size into account) may provide a performance profile that is dependent upon too few of the holdings.

For portfolios designed to hold a mix of both large- and small-sized company stocks, a modified approach might be used to balance concerns about the risk of some of the more speculative holdings. For instance, a portfolio mix of 20 large well-established companies and 5 more speculative companies (e.g. alternative energy stocks) might initially hold 4.5% of each of the 20 large-company stocks. This would leave space for 2.0% of each of the 5 smaller company stocks.

Chapter 4

Fixed Income Investments

A 100% equity investment portfolio is too risky for most investors. Fixed income investments are used to balance the overall risk level of a portfolio. These income investments can be as simple as cash in a savings account, or as complex as an actively-managed bond mutual fund which uses an assortment of strategies that may appear to some as gambling.

In my opinion, many of the basic SRI fixed income investing options would be consistent with a vegan worldview. Here are some examples and comments on some of these options:

Savings Accounts

In general, credit unions or small community banks are preferred over large national banks for savings and checking accounts. Their local focus often provides for a clearer idea of where money is invested (e.g. local home mortgages, home equity loans, auto loans). Note that many credit unions partner with brokerage firms that provide financial planning and investment advisory services that I would *not* classify as low fee providers. Care should be taken regarding the scope of financial services utilized.

CDs

A CD (Certificate of Deposit) from a community bank versus the average large national bank typically provides more assurance about how and where the proceeds are used. Some CDs are named in a way to help you track how the funds are likely to be used (e.g. Sallie Mae in the name would imply the funds are used for college loans). Federally-insured CDs provide a high level of safety (see FDIC.gov and NCUA.gov for information on how federal deposit insurance works). They can be laddered (i.e., 1-year, 2-year, 3-year... maturity dates) to balance out the risk associated with significant changes in interest rates.

Treasury Bonds

Individual treasury bonds or treasury bond funds of appropriate term can be a suitable holding. Term lengths may be short, medium or long depending upon one's objective and view of the direction/rate of interest rate change. Some vegans may see this as relatively neutral from an impact investing perspective. Others may want to avoid them and look at other fixed income options (see IFC Impact Notes).

Calvert Foundation's Community Investment Notes*

These Notes are very popular in the "SRI world" since the funds are used for a variety of social impact purposes in the U.S. and around the world that can be targeted by investors. They are available in various terms (from one to ten years) for as little as $20 online at Vested.org, or $1,000 directly from Calvert Foundation or through a brokerage account. While Calvert Foundation has a 100% repayment rate to investors since 1995, these Notes are not federally insured like a bank or credit union CD. You should have a conversation with your advisor regarding the relative risks and rewards. You can find more information about this investment and the targeted impact options at www.calvertfoundation.org. As of the summer of 2014, some examples of specific targets for investment were microfinance, education, affordable housing, women's empowerment, fair trade, and a growing list of specific cities.

* Disclaimer: Calvert Social Investment Foundation, a 501(c)(3) nonprofit, offers the Community Investment Note, which is subject to certain risks, is not a mutual fund, is not FDIC or SIPC insured, and should not be confused with any Calvert Investments-sponsored investment product. Any decision to invest in these securities should only be made after reading the prospectus or by calling 800.248.0337. Due to Blue Sky regulations, the current offering of the Community Investment Note may not be available in all states.

GNMA Bond Funds

GNMA (Ginnie Mae) bond funds hold a pool of government backed mortgages. Since GNMA bonds have a relatively high safety rating, the rates of return can be lower in comparison with otherwise similar bonds. Given the nature of bond holdings, the bond fund will respond negatively to a rising interest rate environment.

Treasury Inflation Protected Securities (TIPS)

These government-backed bonds can be bought as individual bonds, although they are typically bought as a mutual fund or as an exchange-traded fund in order to provide diversification and convenience. Many financial advisors will recommend some use of TIPS along with other inflation hedges, to help protect purchasing power should the inflation rate increase above modest levels. Younger investors have no first-hand experience or memory of the 1979-1981 years when Social Security payments increased by over 10% per year in response to inflation and interest rate levels. TIPS are used to protect the purchasing power of the funds invested. Significant increases in energy, meat and dairy costs (i.e. movement towards a truer cost) could be expected to contribute to higher-than-normal levels of inflation and make this type of investment helpful.

Inflation Bonds (I-Bonds)

These government-backed bonds can be purchased directly from the US Treasury. Like TIPS, they are designed to be an inflation hedge and provide purchasing power protection should inflation return. TIPS and I-Bonds have different tax treatment, so it is appropriate to consult your financial and/or tax advisor prior to investment. Used correctly, they can provide some tax advantages in addition to providing some inflation insurance. For more information, see http://www.treasurydirect.gov/.

IFC Impact Notes and Green Bonds

The International Finance Corporation (IFC), a member of the World Bank Group, periodically makes available fixed income offerings to institutional and retail investors. A relatively new investment choice, called Impact Notes, provides for a highly-rated (AAA) security that is accessible for as low as $1,000 (note that some brokerage firms may insist on a somewhat higher minimum). See www.ifc.org (search Impact Note) for examples of how funds are used to support positive efforts to address climate change and other areas of likely concern to vegan investors. Some of the maturity and interest step-up features of the Impact Note may help provide diversification in a fixed income portfolio.

At the time of this writing, it is uncertain if the supply of the notes will continue to be sufficient to meet demand.

Clean Energy Victory Bonds (CEVB)

Clean energy victory bonds are not currently available as of the publication date of this book. The site www.cleanenergyvictorybonds.org may provide more information about their current status. The program to establish these bonds requires approval from the US Congress. If and when available, they will provide for a low-entry point ($25 minimum) to fund a host of clean energy programs in the United States. The likely risk/reward proposition may be a helpful fixed income portfolio diversifier for impact investors.

Tax-exempt Municipal Bond Funds and Corporate Bond Funds

You may want to avoid most corporate bond funds since they consist of loans to firms that may not be consistent with your worldview. There are SRI actively managed bond funds that may suit a vegan's needs. However, there are two obstacles. One is that the management fee may eat into your returns in a significant way – this is likely to be a problem for years to come as the long-term interest rate cycle is due to be trending upwards (i.e., relatively low real returns, with "real" being the amount of return you achieve over inflation). Tax-exempt municipal bond funds may be useful depending upon your tax bracket and your risk tolerance. Also, if you have a sufficiently large amount of money to invest, it may be worthwhile to work with an advisor to identify bonds issued by companies that fall within your comfort level. For instance, many of the companies in your stock portfolio may also issue bonds to raise funds for expansion, research and other initiatives.

There is no particular need to own an investment in each sub-class of the fixed income world. If you have a strong need to vegan-bias your investment mix, and you are confident in your worldview, you are not likely to miss much by avoiding other fixed-income investments such as foreign bond funds and currency funds.

Short, Medium or Long Term

Interest rate risk should be taken into careful consideration when investing in fixed income investments. Short-term fixed income investments (e.g., 1-year maturity CD) are less sensitive to the negative effects of rising interest rates while long-term investments (e.g. 10-year treasury bond) can be very sensitive.

In order to illustrate the nature of the risk, consider how you may be positioned with a home mortgage. If you obtain a 30-year mortgage at a very low rate such as 3.5% and interest rates promptly march upwards to 5% in the next few years, you have a very attractive loan cost, especially if rates continue to stay the same or move up from there. The entity that owns the mortgage, however, is not holding a great investment, as they are getting paid back with ever-cheaper dollars.

There is a significant downside to having a strong bias toward short-term bonds or bond funds. The bonds are inevitably priced to take the risk/reward proposition into account. This is evident when comparing 1-year CD rates with 3- or 5-year CD rates.

In order to balance the risks involved, the more-familiar concept of a CD ladder (e.g., a mix of 1-, 2-,3-,4- and 5-year CDs) may be applied to your fixed income portfolio. Financial planners and investment advisors typically have access to information or software tools that can assess the amount of interest rate risk present.

In some cases fixed income investments with a positive social element provide less income (i.e., dividends or interest) than a similar financial service product without a social benefit. For instance, a bond that collects funds to support a clear social cause will often be designed to benefit that particular cause (borrower) with a lower cost of funds, with the thought that the investor is not seeking purely a financial return on investment.

High and Low Quality

Fixed income investments have various levels of default risk that result from the quality of the loan. Government-guaranteed and international agency fixed income investments are considered high in quality, as there is little risk of default. Investment in a fund that holds high-yield (i.e. high- risk) bonds can produce great returns when all goes well, but result in losses in less favorable circumstances.

The amount of risk in the fixed income portion of your overall portfolio is an important consideration and depends on your capacity for risk. I find that many financial planners tend to recommend designing the fixed income portion of a portfolio to be relatively low risk and to use the equity/fixed income ratio of the portfolio to adjust the overall risk level.

Chapter 5

Alternative Investments

This chapter covers investments other than stocks, bonds and cash that may be of interest to a vegan investor.

Human Capital

For some, how they spend their time, what they work at (job) or work towards (education) represents their largest investment. Although financial capital is the main focus of this book, human capital (intellectual, social and spiritual) is an important consideration.

Employment

If planning for a first or new career, my perspective as a financial planner has made it clear that there is a unique gratification when a person's work aligns with his or her values and worldview. All too often the motivation to see a financial planner is based on job disruption or dissatisfaction (i.e., when can I retire?). One of the happiest meetings financial planners can have is when they can illustrate to a client that their financial freedom point has been achieved. In other words, the client can work at what they want to do for the remainder of their lives.

One alternative, therefore, is to take the time to explore a career path that would be directly or indirectly consistent with a worldview. Some of the larger cities have annual vegan fairs that illustrate many of the manufacturing and service sector opportunities that are available in an area where there is a high likelihood of steadily growing demand and appreciation.

Starting a business or investing in a business might be a great option for those with the means or an entrepreneurial spirit. For some investors of sufficient means, there are opportunities to participate in the funding of a vegan business venture (e.g. vegan restaurant franchise or independent). The amount of funds allocated to business investment should typically be considered as part of a speculative portion of one's portfolio. In this context, I would define speculative as the portion of funds that are not needed to fund one's financial goals. In other words, you can afford a total loss, both financially and mentally.

Organic Farmland

For some high-net-worth investors, direct ownership of farmland used to grow organic vegetables can be very satisfying. In many cases it is not advisable, practical or possible to do this. There are several possible approaches that can be used to support the continued growth of this sector.

One of the simplest approaches, when available, is to support local organic farmers via their supermarket or farmers' market. Supermarket advertisements may note the vegetables that are sourced locally to spare you a lot of research.

Another approach, again when available, is to purchase a membership in a local CSA (community supported agriculture) cooperative. Seasoned vegans are probably well aware of this option, as local fresh produce makes for tastier meals.

There is another approach available to high-net-worth investors who prefer to invest a significant, but measured, amount into organic farmland. In this context, it is important to introduce the term "accredited investor" to more specifically define a high net worth investor. To qualify by net worth, an individual (or married couple) needs to have $1,000,000 or more in assets (not including the value of their primary residence). To qualify by income, an individual's income needs to exceed $200,000 per year in each of the past two most recent years ($300,000 for a married couple) and reasonably be expected to meet this level for the current year.

Firms such as Iroquois Valley Farm and Farmland LP facilitate the investment in the conversion of typical farmland into organic farmland.[22,23] It is very important to note that these farms typically have a non-vegan livestock component to them. For some vegans, the incremental environmental improvement in agricultural practice might represent a tolerable investment. For others, it would be best to avoid until the day comes when a vegan-friendlier variation of this investment opportunity exists.

It is extremely important to keep in mind that an indirect investment in farmland should still be viewed as a long-term investment, and that all of the risks and tax considerations need to be taken into account.

Solar Energy

The growth in solar panel installation over the past several years has produced a remarkable opportunity for some investors, and a rough ride or disaster for others. Rapid growth in market and technology still make holding the stocks of solar companies a relatively high-risk investment. Diversification in a fair number of companies in this sector can bring down the risk level into the range where some investors can consider a modest allocation (i.e., small percentage of overall investment assets) to a collection of stocks in this sector.

Solar Funding

For accredited investors, there is a mechanism to fund one or more solar projects and collect an income stream from that investment (see joinmosaic.com). Of course, even accredited investors need to be careful of the risks involved -- and should be careful with the percentage of their wealth they direct to this type of investment.

There is likely to be a growing number of crowd-funding options to support solar projects available to accredited and non-accredited investors alike. This is an area to review with an advisor.

Direct Solar, Wind or Geothermal Investment

The prices of installing sustainable energy systems in a home or business have dropped to a point where they can provide an attractive investment alternative. The viability of a clean energy project should take all relevant factors into consideration. For instance, a residential PV (photovoltaic) solar project should take into account the following:

- Are you likely to be staying in your home for a long enough time to see the benefits? Alternatively, would a new buyer in your area appreciate the amenity and price that into their purchase decision?
- Do the federal, state or local incentive programs currently in effect provide for a reasonable payback period?
- Does the sunlight estimate for your installation make the project viable? Will there be young trees nearby that may eventually reduce the sunlight available during the multi-decade lifecycle of the project?
- Is your roof in good enough condition to justify the investment? If not, does an upgrade to a long-life roofing material make sense (e.g. optimum timing would be to have a

re-roofing project coincide with the PV panel installation)?

- Can your roof support the additional weight of solar panels? A review by a structural engineer may be needed as part of the permitting process.
- Does your power company buy back power?
- What is the likelihood that electric power rates will continue to rise in your area (i.e. does your community have any locked in long-term contracts)?

Although this is only a partial list of considerations, you should not be discouraged. A good contractor should be able to provide you with information regarding the estimated return on investment since annual sunlight data for given locations is available.

When evaluating the return on investment, the rate should be looked at in view of comparable returns on safe, long-term investments. Also, in many cases, it can be assumed that electricity costs will increase at the inflation rate, or higher. Thus a solar panel installation could represent a significant hedge against a major boost in electricity prices.

Loans

For investors of significant means, interest-bearing loans to conservancy organizations (e.g., Nature Conservancy) may be an attractive option. Although the use of outright gifts and donations of cash or securities is even more appreciated by such organizations, some may be interested in other mutually beneficial financial arrangements.

Charitable Gift Annuities (CGA)

If you are in need of a fixed annuity product, you may be able to arrange a CGA with an organization that you support (see Chapter 11 for more information on faith-based CGAs). Some financial planners recommend a fixed annuity to clients without pensions and/or limited Social Security income

Chapter 6

Taxes

The impact of taxes on an investment strategy can be significant. Some investments are considered tax-efficient while others are not. For instance, the use of tax-deferred accounts (401(k), IRA) can defer taxation, while taxable accounts (e.g. savings accounts, taxable brokerage accounts) generate annual income or losses which must be included on your annual tax return.

Along with the general approach being taken in this book, vegan investors may want to balance the ideal considerations (what tax policy they would like to see in the present and future) versus more pragmatic ones (what tax policy is and may realistically be in the future as their worldview unfolds). Although there is an urgent need for healthier people and a healthier planet, it is realistic to assume that a vegan worldview will not be established quickly. Fortunately, however, the current growth rate and popularity of better food choices is likely sufficient to positively impact an investing strategy that takes this trend into account.[24]

As you may be aware, there is movement in the direction of putting a price on carbon. One mechanism that has a reasonable chance of becoming reality is a revenue-neutral tax on carbon.[17] Certain equity sectors (e.g., big oil) are likely to lose some of the tax advantages they have. Or, at a minimum, the playing field may be leveled. For instance, master limited partnerships (MLPs) have favorable tax treatment for oil and pipeline projects. As climate change awareness increases, this sector may be at a disadvantage and good to avoid. Also, more direct carbon taxes (at the source) will not be a positive for carbon producers. By avoiding such sectors, a mix tilted toward a vegan worldview may have a relative advantage.

Certain traditional utility providers may also be negatively impacted, especially those that rely heavily on coal.[25]

Taxes on soft drinks and high-sugar products will likely be an ongoing focus. First, the need for government/tax revenue continues to grow. Second, the externalized cost for unhealthy food choices is becoming more apparent.

Externalized Cost

It is reasonable to look at the future direction of tax policy when establishing a long-term investment policy or worldview that is consistent with your values. It is helpful to look at how capturing externalized cost could have an impact. Several examples may be helpful to illustrate the concept.

In the summer of 2014, over 400,000 residents near Toledo, Ohio were advised against drinking the water supplied by the local utility. An algae bloom in Lake Erie released the toxin microcystin at levels considered hazardous to human health. Residents and businesses suffered various degrees of financial loss as alternative sources of water needed to be used for several days. The cause of the event was linked to nitrogen and phosphorous levels contained in runoff from farms that surround Lake Erie. Climate change due to increased greenhouse gas levels could not be ruled out as a contributing cause. Regardless of the specific cause, the cost of the event was not easily billable to those who contributed to the problem and benefited from not having to capture the waste they put into the environment.

An even more vegan-specific example of externalized cost is seen in how vegan taxpayers foot the bill for the consequences of the poor food choices of others. The excess amount of greenhouse gases generated by meat and dairy use place the cost of climate disruption on all. Meat and dairy industries do not currently pay for the significant excess of greenhouse gases they produce as a by-product. The cost is externalized to others, whether we use their products or not.

As health care expenses increase with an aging population, the pharmaceutical sector typically benefits as a result of sales growth. Tax policy tends to look for where the money is and the tendency to take back some of this revenue is always present. This risk could temper investor enthusiasm for an otherwise logical reason to favor investment in this sector.

Companies introducing new green technology are likely to have some tax incentives. Of course, opposing moneyed interests may continue to provide a strong fight. As the saying goes, however, nothing is stronger than an idea whose time has come. The narrative of sustainability continues to grow in a world where information moves quickly and broadly.

As might be expected, many important tax planning issues and opportunities are independent of the investment selection strategy employed. Therefore, in most cases, traditional tax strategies should be used in consultation with your financial advisor and tax professional.

Chapter 7

Putting It All Together

For most, it is difficult to imagine an investment mix that is in 100% alignment with our worldview. If you work for the government or a large employer, your 401(k) or retirement plan choices are probably limited. If you are lucky, you have access to low cost index funds and perhaps even a broad-scoped socially responsible fund. For those in retirement or not restricted by such limitations, more self-directed investments are possible.

The process of balancing between cash, stock and bond holdings is referred to as *asset allocation*. For money with a long time horizon (i.e., not likely to be spent for at least 10 years), investment in a significant amount (e.g. 40%, 50%, 60% ...) of stocks is often appropriate. Use of cash, or cash-like investments, provides a suitable amount of safety for money with a short time horizon. Bonds are used to fill the middle bucket – they provide some return to keep up with inflation and typically provide for less uncertainty than stocks.

A young investor (just starting out) or an investor with modest means may not be in a position to invest in anything more than a savings account. An emergency fund in an account with a credit union or community bank may be all that is feasible.

The next level of investment opportunity often involves participation in an employer-provided retirement plan. None (to my knowledge) have vegan mutual fund options. Some have reasonably well-rated socially responsible investment mutual funds and these could be more satisfying than a more generic index fund or actively managed fund. If there is a strong desire to have a vegan tilt, you may want to limit your employer retirement plan participation up to the maximum match that is being provided. Then, you can direct any additional available savings to areas where you have much more control over the specific investment selections.

If you are saving for educational expenses using a 529 plan, again, your options are limited and it may be appropriate to take the potential tax benefits of the 529 plan over the alternative of control over your choices.

If you are in a position to utilize self-funded and managed accounts, you are in a position to buy equity and fixed income investments that fit into the suggested screening criteria. Balancing simplicity, investment cost, and effectiveness in meeting your goals should be a primary consideration.

For higher net worth investors, the number of options can grow to include many of the suggested possibilities. I would encourage avoiding too much complexity of the overall investment mix unless this is an area that you enjoy and have the time and energy to stay on top of. As an hourly advisor, I find that even an annual review interval arrives much too quickly for most lifestyles. A bias towards the simple side allows for the review period to be stretched a bit without a significant downside.

Organizations often have short-, medium- and long-term documented plans to guide their decisions. For individuals and families, a financial plan can be used for this purpose as well. Incorporating your vegan values into your financial plan can maximize the satisfaction you derive from your lifestyle choices.

Chapter 8

Does It Really Matter?

You are only one drop in a very large ocean. The same argument might be used for not voting. Although individual investors may feel that their impact is insignificant, it is important to point out that one out of every six dollars under professional management in the United States is invested according to SRI strategies -- and that is trending up. According to *The Forum for Sustainable and Responsible Investment's* "Report on US Sustainable, Responsible and Impact Investing Trends 2014," there was a growth rate of 77% from 2012 to 2014.[26] It is likely that the percentage of socially screened investment will continue to increase.

In order to address the question of how investment dollars translate to a company's capabilities, limitations and behavior, it may be helpful to illustrate how stocks and bonds work – and why your actions can have influence. The following story is not about an actual company, the company names and products are also fictitious. Any resemblance to actual companies or products is coincidental.

The Fable of Food, ILC

Once upon a time, many years ago, a town butcher was looking for a good use for a lot of waste animal fat and by-products. His brother, the town baker, decided to take some of the material, mix it with sugar, salt and a small amount of plant-based material and bake it. To the brothers' surprise, the resulting product tasted pretty good. With a little more research and tweaking of the recipe and presentation, they found that it tasted *very* good - almost addicting. They decided to offer the product for sale and, as you might expect, they became quite successful and word of their discovery spread.

The brothers soon met someone who was in a position to turn their product into a national sensation. They sold the recipe and rights to the product to an individual who had the skill set to expand the business rapidly and effectively. The brothers received a million dollars each and were given part time jobs as company consultants for the next few years before their early retirement. A new company, Food, ILC, was formed (ILC stands for Infinite Liability Corporation and is an invented term to advance the story line).

The company needed money to expand. The chief financial officer of Food, ILC arranged for a stock offering of 1 million shares of company stock at a price of $10 each. The stockholders became the owners of the company, entitled to share in the future growth and profitability of the company. In order to double the amount of money for the expansion, $10 million in bonds were also issued. Since the company was brand new and therefore a higher risk, the interest rate on the bond was set relatively high. The bondholders became entitled to the agreed-upon interest rate for the agreed-upon period of time.

Time passed and the product was a success. A second shift was added at the manufacturing facilities, sales and profit were more than enough to comfortably pay the bondholders and even provided a nice dividend to the stockholders. Food, ILC management reviewed their situation and decided that a quantum leap in expansion was the next logical step. To fund the expansion, they needed to issue *more* stock and borrow *more* money (i.e. issue more bonds). The existing shareholders were confident in the success of the product, and were not concerned with a potential dilution of value as the money was being put to good use. *As a matter of fact, they and the new shareholders were so pleased with the prospects of the company that they were more than happy to buy the new shares, so much so that the price of the shares rose in relative value with each passing month (i.e., if the prospects for future growth and profits are good, the value of a share moves up to what the law of supply and demand ultimately dictates).* The new bondholders were happy to accept a lower interest rate on the new notes being issued: the prospects of the company were good and their track record was well-established, so there was less risk of default.

As time went on, new combinations of animal fat, sugar, salt and a dash of plant-based food, were developed, new plants built, and Food, ILC even expanded into new areas to diversify its product portfolio – always funded by a combination of profits, new stock and new bonds.

Food, ILC grew to become a large company of critical mass and was added as a holding of a major stock index (e.g., the S&P 500 index). Almost overnight, many fund managers were compelled to buy shares of the company, whether they wanted to or not. Index funds are not static in their composition and change to reflect the economic landscape.

How this fable developed and ends can depend on investors.

What are your choices if you do not want to own Food, ILC? A screened portfolio is often seen as a pragmatic solution since not owning any publicly held stock is not a viable solution to many.

What could happen to the fate of a company that is screened out by investors? Simply, the law of supply and demand can, and does, kick in. If there are more sellers than buyers for a stock on a particular day, the price of the stock trends lower. This negative momentum does not place the company in a great position to expand by selling new shares. Such a move might even cause existing shareholders to reevaluate their need to hold the stock. New bond issues are not likely to be set at attractive interest rates for a company that is losing public favor.

One argument against social screens it that this action just provides a higher share of the company profits to those buying the depressed shares and it all evens itself out. This point is valid, provided the company remains profitable. Investor demand, however is typically related to the prospects of a company. In the case of Food, ILC, socially motivated investors might expect that, eventually, the products of Food, ILC will fall out of favor with consumers. Alternatively, the management of Food, ILC might respond to socially active investors (and those who choose to sell and walk away) by using some of their profits, financial horsepower and capacity to move toward healthier products.

Bottom line: your investment dollars talk.

There are some areas where share ownership is an appropriate mechanism to drive change of a company. Ownership enables proxy voting rights, attending meetings and being an activist investor. On the other hand, if one's worldview is to avoid meat and dairy products, there is no point in engaging the company – asking them to shut down their business is unrealistic. This issue is currently being played out in the fossil fuel divestment area. Some argue that shareholder engagement (and therefore holding shares) allows an investor group to ask for incremental improvements (e.g., perhaps capturing more excess pollution). Others argue that the business model of many of the fossil fuel providers is to continue to develop and search for more fossil fuel sources than can ever be safely consumed. Since business models gravitate towards self-preservation of the entity (e.g., lobby dollars used to thwart carbon-free energy alternatives), a "starve the beast" (divestment) approach tends to be accepted by vegan investors.

It is helpful to recognize when shareholder activism is applicable and when simple avoidance is the better choice.

CHAPTER 9

QUESTIONS AND ANSWERS

Here are some anticipated questions and corresponding answers regarding a low fee approach to vegan investing. Some of these questions are either repeated from *Low Fee Socially Responsible Investing* or are appropriately updated.

1. A portfolio of 25 to 30 stocks does not seem representative of any existing index, and performance cannot be easily benchmarked. Is this a problem?

This is true, but keep in mind that your worldview is the primary consideration and that you should be prepared to use this approach completely or, in part, in accordance with your investment objective. This is one of the primary reasons why I believe you should use this approach with the assistance of an advisor who can review the proposed portfolio in the full context of your financial position, in the same way as they would look at any other collection of stocks you may own. As an advisor, I have observed that a number of individual investors come to me holding portfolios consisting of even fewer stocks that may or may not reflect their social preferences. In cases such as this, diversification to 20 to 50 stocks significantly reduces the risk.

Many popular stocks in SRI portfolios are those of very large companies (large cap stocks). A significant number of stocks are even part of the 30-stock Dow Jones Industrial Average (the Dow:DJIA), and it is likely that many portfolios generated will consist of stocks of large and mid-sized companies which have a general tendency to track two of the most popular indices, the Dow and the S&P 500. Again, the primary purpose of the portfolio is to reflect your worldview.

Note that index investing relies on a slow and steady redefinition of what stocks are "in." For instance, in

2013, Facebook (FB) was added to the S&P 500 index and Teradyne was taken out.[27] Sometimes a stock is taken out of the index as a result of a company moving from public into private hands. Sometimes the company is shrinking in economic significance. Mergers and acquisition activity impacts the definition of the index as well. Bottom line – it is important to recognize the index is not as fixed a benchmark as one might think!

2. Will a portfolio that avoids some major sectors of the economy behave unpredictably and be harmful to my finances?

Although my experience with ultra-low fee portfolios developed to date does not indicate unusual behavior, it is indeed possible that a vegan-inspired portfolio could produce disappointing results. I believe the role of the advisor is to help you develop an overall portfolio in line with your expectations. You and your advisor should jointly review appropriate historical data for the proposed portfolio using standard analytical tools. More importantly, the portfolio can be watched for a period of time before a single dollar is invested.

3. Does a dollar-weighted allocation produce a disadvantage relative to market-weighted portfolios?

Since the portfolio contains a relatively small number of stocks, there is a balance to be struck between tracking the overall market and the safety provided by limiting the maximum percentage to one single stock to not more than 5.0%. The use of several themes (i.e., mixes of 20 to 30 stocks each), can help provide a satisfactory amount of diversification.

4. What are the risks of maintaining a portfolio that is not actively managed?

There is a significant amount of evidence to illustrate that passive investing provides for better results over active management and that fee drag associated with active management is a problem.[17] Note that any legally obtained company news that could impact a stock price is not likely to be successfully acted upon by active fund managers, in that their timing would have to be immediate and correct in the long-term. If you have a positive view of active management, it would be better for you to be introduced to one of the many actively managed funds that are available that might approximate your worldview. If you are aware of the academic and published data that supports passive management yet have a strong desire for having your investments reflect your worldview, then a low-fee approach should be of interest to you, provided you have investable assets of sufficient size to make the effort worthwhile.

Most companies do not change their product line or behavior that rapidly. An annual portfolio evaluation and rebalance is likely to offer a reasonable balance between investment cost and objective.

5. Will an investor-defined portfolio make it difficult for an investment advisor to structure an overall portfolio that is considered well-balanced?

It is difficult to define "well-balanced" in view of the diversity of passive and managed portfolios that are already available. If you and your advisor are more concerned with theoretical portfolio balance at just about any cost, this approach is not for you. If you are comfortable with a less rigid approach to portfolio construction, you may want to study this option to determine if a certain significant reduction in investment expense more than offsets the potential theoretical impact of some imbalance. Of course, both you and your advisor should consider appropriate ways to achieve reasonable balance, at a reasonable cost, by partially utilizing other low-fee funds.

6. How would I find an advisor willing to utilize this approach?

There are investment advisors across the country and world who, upon reading this short book and its predecessor, will understand how to implement this approach to impact investing. There may be some advisors willing to implement this approach, but who may not want to be bothered with the portfolio construction process. In this instance, they can subcontract the portfolio construction to an advisor interested in this work. I am already aware of a number of fellow members of the Garrett Planning Network who are interested in this portfolio development approach, as it fits well with their hourly fee-only practice. I anticipate that other fee-only advisors outside of the Garrett Planning Network would be willing to provide this service, provided their business model or practice allows them to offer it.

7. How can a low fee portfolio construction cost be assured, since advisors have a wide range of fees?

There is no absolute assurance that you will be able to find an advisor who is willing to embrace this low-fee model. Also, a vegan worldview may prove to be too restrictive to allow for efficient construction by some advisors. The construction process is, however, relatively simple and one that can be mastered in a short period of time. It is hoped that market forces will be at work, and an increasing number of advisors will become proficient at this approach and not keep the availability of this service a secret.

8. How can low portfolio maintenance cost be assured since various discount brokerage firms and investment management firms have different cost structures?

The first step is to check with your current investment custodian and work with an advisor to determine if you will be able to implement this strategy in a cost-efficient manner, without the inconvenience of having to move some of your assets onto another platform. If this does not work, I have already mentioned two low-fee custodians that could be considered (Motif Investing and Folio Investing®). Stock trading fees are under constant pressure downwards so you should be able to find a trading platform that works for you (e.g. a stock portfolio of 50 stocks, traded at $7 per trade, is still only $350 per year, provided that you make purchases or sales only once per year).

9. If I work with an advisor to generate a portfolio of 30 to 60 stocks, is it okay if I buy them over the course of time or buy only the specific stocks I really like first?

The objective is to obtain the benefits of a disciplined approach to low fee, passive investing and utilize a sufficient amount of diversification to manage investment risk. Buying the stocks as a group may better achieve these objectives.

10. Would it be reasonable to buy the portfolio of stocks when the market appears to be undervalued and/or sell the portfolio of stocks if the market appears to be somewhat pricey?

The same discipline used when buying a collection of mutual funds or exchange traded funds for the long-term would apply. There may be some circumstances where market valuation levels may be taken into consideration (e.g. during periods near rebalancing, introduction of significant new investment dollars, or tax loss harvesting).

11. Regarding taxes - what are some of the tax considerations for this approach versus a mutual fund investment?

Since this approach uses portfolios that are a collection of individual stocks rather than a mutual fund you have a significant advantage over a mutual fund investor, in that mutual fund capital gain distributions are not always predictable and within the control of the investor. Though messy in a taxable account (e.g. scores of entries on a Schedule D), this approach would allow for some tax planning. In a tax-deferred account, there is no significant tax planning difference that I am aware of.

12. Is it appropriate to consider constructing and investing in several small stock mixes as part of an overall portfolio of stocks?

It is appropriate for many investors to consider the use of several mixes. A group of large company stocks can be used to provide stability and near-benchmark performance while a collection of smaller company stocks can be used, partly, to add a growth or a more speculative element.

13. What are the benefits in addition to lower investment cost?

In addition to the benefits already noted, such as potential tax planning opportunities and aligning your investments with your values, consider the impact on your behavior as an investor. As much as both investors and advisors try to believe they can be immune to emotional reactions to market volatility, there appears to be little evidence to support much success in this regard. Although I make no claim of credentials as a psychologist, it would seem reasonable to expect that you would be more likely to stand firm in volatile times with an investment set representing your worldview than with a set of investments to which you have less connection. As previously noted, a vegan worldview, by definition, requires a fair amount of commitment. Of course, it is up to both you and your advisor to ease into this investment approach so that it becomes a source of stability, and not uncertainty.

From a standpoint of SRI, one of the common criticisms of mutual fund investing is that there is no assurance that an investor's viewpoint is being represented in any proxy votes that take place in a given company whose stock is being held. By holding individual stocks, any proxy voting materials can be directly acted upon by you, the investor. Better yet, by holding stock only in companies that are screened in accordance with your values, there will likely be fewer controversial proxy issues of concern.

If during the course of time, you become aware of some attributes of a company whose stock you are holding that disturbs you, you have the ability to consider redefining the screening criteria. Rather than being negatively impacted by the unexpected consequences of arbitrary decisions on the selection and purchase timing of individual stocks, changes of investment preferences can be treated in a systematic manner.

14. What if I really like the idea of investing per my vegan worldview but do not have enough to invest to make it cost effective?

If you do not have the resources to pursue a custom-built portfolio, you may find an existing low fee exchange traded fund (ETF), Motif or Folio® that meets at least some of your preferences (e.g., a general social index fund versus a broad index fund. Refer to each brokerage firm's current account size minimum requirements.

15. Would there be a significant cost saving if I use an existing portfolio that an advisor has already established to address a given set of values/perspectives?

There may be. This may represent an ideal situation and the costs may be lower. Note, however, that portfolio documentation should be reviewed by both you and your advisor in order to ensure that it meets your investment objectives. If you are already working with an advisor utilizing this approach and choose to direct some of your funds into an existing model, the incremental cost to use this approach may be even lower.

16. How likely is it that a 20- to 60-stock portfolio will track one of the established benchmarks?

In recent history, stock prices of many companies have tended to move up and down together, and a 20- to 60-stock portfolio is likely to provide sufficient correlation to demonstrate a fair amount of market tracking. Given the multitude of indices and benchmarks, I would maintain that attempting to track a given benchmark is, in essence, also akin to taking a worldview position. If for instance, you decide that your objective is to track the S&P 500, a large collection of stocks - your worldview is that satisfactory long-term investment performance is defined as capturing the returns of holding a market-weighted basket of stocks representative of a generally accepted approach to measure economic activity. Of course, the benchmarks themselves are not fixed and stocks are added and subtracted periodically. It is important to note that the discipline of diversification, limited modifications and periodic rebalancing of the index contributes to relatively satisfactory results. Any given index does not have a certain claim to superior performance over any other index. Tracking a benchmark is no assurance of positive or superior returns versus any other particular worldview. Therefore, it would appear that the benefit to be obtained is the discipline rather than replication of the allocation represented in the benchmark.

It typically takes a very long time to determine which model or benchmark will produce optimal performance. For instance, what does it imply when an active fund manager dismisses his 1- year and 3-year performance data when he is below the benchmark, noting that his 10 year record is over the benchmark? What is the appropriate time horizon to measure performance? From your perspective, it could be your lifetime if you plan on holding the investment and passing it on to heirs. Or it could be until you plan on using the invested funds for something else in 5 to 10 years time.

17. What if the "sin" stocks outperform the benchmarks over the long-term?

If this occurs over the time horizon of interest, you would have been better off financially investing in the "sin" stocks or a fund that contains these stocks. Of course, the future performance of this group or any group of stocks is unknown. It is clear, however, that the popularity of socially responsible investing is steadily growing and that momentum would appear to favor stocks of companies that are aligned with this significant trend. If your vegan worldview is correct, then an effort to screen accordingly might be rewarding on yet another level.

Chapter 10

For Advisors

Although investors are encouraged to read this chapter, this information is geared toward the advisor.

The basic equity portfolio construction process is outlined in my book, *Low Fee Socially Responsible Investing*.

If your practice allows you to use a discount brokerage platform that facilitates purchase and ownership of partial shares of stock, you are in a position to offer low fee vegan investing to your clients. Depending upon the size of your client's portfolio, it may be possible to achieve a low-fee result using other platforms (i.e., rounding to the nearest full share).

If you are a member of a fee only advisor network, such as the Garrett Planning Network, Inc., or the National Association of Personal Financial Advisors (NAPFA), you may be familiar with advisors who offer socially responsible investing solutions to their clients and who may be willing to share passive portfolio tools with you, provided you take full responsibility for how these may be used by your clients (i.e., maintain full fiduciary responsibility and be in a position to verify, maintain and generate updated portfolios, if needed).

Additional ideas that may be of interest to some of your clients interested in a vegan investment worldview can be found at www.lowfeesociallyresponsibleinvesting.com.

If you are an advisor who would like to serve vegan impact investors, it is recommended that you reach out to other advisors who share this interest.

If you are not already familiar with the area of socially responsible investing, I recommend you consider joining The Forum for Sustainable and Responsible Investment (US SIF). This organization has annual conferences, provides training classes and access to an active member discussion forum. In some locations, you may find regional discussion groups of like-minded advisors.[26]

If your business is not already certified by Green America, you may want to consider this to document your commitment to many of the principles embraced by vegan and green investors.[28]

If you are not already familiar with typical vegan values that might help inform investment selection preferences, I recommend you add several of the books mentioned in the bibliography to your reading list. Would you rather watch a movie? Documentaries such as: Food Inc (2008), Vegucated (2010),
Fat, Sick & Nearly Dead (2010) and Forks Over Knives (2011) will help get you up to speed. If you prefer to learn more about veganism through humor, take a look at www.veganstreet.com and sign up for the weekly newsletter. If you still have an appetite for more information, then view the video clips provided on Dr. McDougall's website: www.drmcdougall.com.

Investment Process

As you are aware, client assets in employer retirement accounts do not typically contain choices that fit into a client's worldview. Also, choices may be so limited as to make it difficult to optimize your recommendations (e.g., limited range of fixed income investments, funds with high fees, etc.). Depending upon the depth of your client's convictions, you may want to tilt the employer retirement portfolio to allow relatively more equity in the taxable or self-manageable IRA accounts. The use of stable value funds in a 401(k) account may offer a "lesser of other evils" solution. As an advisor, it is important to not promise a perfect vegan investing portfolio and not engage to work with anyone who requires more accuracy and precision than what can be delivered.

For many investors and advisors, the convenience of established or customized Folios® or Motifs is an attractive option due to the low investment fees. Appropriate time should be invested to assure that expectations are clear.

Many advisors, myself included, recognize the attraction of a simple, yet effective, collection of index funds to meet an investor's needs. The success and growth of index fund usage in the past decade or so establishes their use as a safe harbor, if nothing else. This safeness, provides for a combination of both fear and risk management. By fear management, I refer to the fear that other investors and advisors who utilize only index funds, will achieve better performance and less volatility. Impact or vegan investors need to have sufficient commitment to their worldview to put aside this fear.

Risk management (versus fear management and maximum diversification) is the focus for advisors and their impact investor clients. By definition, the low fee vegan investor will not have a portfolio representative of all sectors of the economy or asset classes. As advisors, many of us develop a belief that helping a client manage a portfolio of individual stocks requires us to be experts in the area of stock picking and timing. I believe the key is to utilize the principles of sound, passive investing and not assume the approach I am recommending requires stock picking expertise or active management. In a disciplined, well-defined, screening process, the stocks pick themselves.

Many advisors have read at least one book by or about Warren Buffet and are familiar with his preference for index versus active investing, given only the two choices. Of course, he personally follows a third strategy that is referred to as "focus investing". This approach relies on a relatively small number of holdings, a long-term holding period, acceptance of volatility, and owning high-quality companies that you can truly understand – an approach that seems adaptable to vegan investing.[29]

The overall approach described in this book is to take advantage of sufficient diversification, sufficient discipline, appropriate insight, passive management and low fees. As Jack Bogle, the founder of Vanguard, often states "costs matter, keep them low".[30]

Depending upon the portfolio evaluation tool you use (e.g. Morningstar®), I recommend that you evaluate portfolios that fit the descriptions I have mentioned. Alternatively, review the historical data of some established portfolios of 50 or fewer stocks (either equally or market-weighted). Your first reaction might be that the result is not as scary as you initially imagined. Better yet, look at a listing of the largest 100 publicly listed stocks and pick 30 stocks that you believe (based on your reading of Chapter 3) might be acceptable to a vegan investor. I anticipate you will see a performance and volatility profile that is not much off the benchmark.

Now consider how this could be improved upon by a few more filters. First, filter out companies that are not generally found in SRI mutual funds or ETFs (there tends to more agreement of what is and what is not SRI than you may initially have thought). Next, filter out companies that have relatively weaker financial positions over their peers (e.g., stick to top 40%). Since financial rankings or a company's fortune may change quickly, the operating assumption is that stronger companies are more likely to endure. Equally weight the mix to minimize the downside risk of one "bad apple". Finally, commit to review/rebalance the mix on an annual basis. Perfect? No way! Good? Maybe.

I mentioned in the *Introduction* that I was not aware of any published data ranking publicly traded companies on their appeal to vegan values. This may change at some future point and open up the possibility of a simpler and widely recognized standard. In studying the projects being taken by Dr. Richard Oppenlander, author of *Comfortably Unaware*, and *Food Choice and Sustainability*, his website, www.inspireawarenessnow.org, may someday include detailed rankings and metrics on companies included in the S&P 500. This information, combined with one or two additional screens (e.g., financial position ranking), has the potential to more clearly define the criteria for vegan impact investing.

Chapter 11

For Vegan Investors

If you are an experienced investor, you may already be familiar with many of the ideas presented in this book. I hope you have found some new ideas or at least confirmation of some of the investment strategies that you are already using.

Most (if not all) readers of this book will want to have the help of a financial advisor before moving forward on a vegan investment plan. Chances are your current investment advisor, if not already utilizing the concept of impact or sustainable investing, will meet your interest in vegan investing with a familiar eye roll (you know, the one you sometimes get when you mention you are a vegan to a new acquaintance). This is to be expected. The literature on vegan investing is almost non-existent for reasons already mentioned.

If your current investment advisor gets paid on the basis of financial product he sells, you are not likely to get a warm reception as he may not have anything in his inventory. As mentioned, as far as I can tell, there are no vegan-themed mutual funds or exchange traded funds. Your current advisor may be able to assist with some of the fixed income ideas. In some cases, you may not want to make substantial changes at first and may be able to reach an investment mix that works out well for both you and your advisor.

If your current investment advisor gets paid on a percentage of the assets you have invested (e.g., 1% of your portfolio per year; 1% of $500,000 = $5,000 per-year-fee subtracted from your account), he has an incentive to want to keep you as a client. Some advisors have a fairly rigid mix of what they manage and will resist your request and try to talk you out of such an unfamiliar strategy. Others may be able to provide a very satisfactory amount of support by incorporating some of the vegan-themed ideas that appeal to you and suit your financial circumstances.

If your advisor is not familiar with socially responsible, sustainable investing or impact investing, you may get significant resistance. Until they learn otherwise, most advisors believe many of the myths surrounding sustainable investing and have not taken time to investigate the benefits. You may hear them talk about the lack of diversity, poor performance, higher fees, and a lack of clarity as to the objective. All of these issues were addressed in my first book but also apply to the more specific criteria of vegan investing.

The current interest in fossil-free divestment is expanding public awareness into the area of socially responsible investing and, if nothing else, financial advisors are familiar with the principle of supply and demand. The amount of advisors available to meet your needs is surely going to grow. The connection between climate and vegan investment goals makes it more likely than ever that you will be able to identify someone who is willing and able to work with you.

If your advisor is familiar with socially responsible investing, it is likely that your interest in vegan investing will capture her interest. As noted, vegan investing shares many of the objectives of those concerned with climate change. The number of investment solutions available to address fossil fuel divestment was very limited up until 2013. The number of options added within a year's time was significant and is still growing. It is reasonable to expect that vegan-inspired investment solutions could grow as well.

As noted in the introduction, a low fee vegan investment approach works well with an advisor who is paid on an hourly basis (or by a retainer that is based on the amount of time used per year). There are a growing number of hourly fee-only financial advisors aware of, if not familiar with, many of the ideas presented. At a minimum, they should be able to point you in the right direction. More likely, they will be able to help you meet most, if not all, of your needs. Remember that the principle of supply and demand is in your favor – if enough customers demand low fee vegan investment solutions, the supply of service providers will grow to meet the need.

If you currently do not use an investment advisor, then you may seriously want to consider the benefits of, at a minimum, a second opinion.

Chapter 12

Faith-based Vegan Investing

Faith-motivated investment screening is one of the earliest examples of socially responsible or impact investing. Avoiding investment in companies involved in the production and use of alcohol is one of the first (and still relevant) examples. Since food choice is often a key element in religious observance and practice, it is very appropriate to carry these values into one's personal investing selections.

In addition to vegan values, it is possible that your faith, if relevant, may further influence both equity and fixed income investments that are best suited to you. Of course, this influence may be a strong or weak case depending upon your faith, your targeted level of compliance and the precepts of the faith, itself.

Rather than attempt to summarize the existing literature on faith and vegan food choice, the primary focus in this chapter is to reinforce how this topic is relevant to the vegan investor looking for relatively low fee approaches. A relatively comprehensive collection of writings and quotes on the topic can be found on a website maintained by the Society of Ethical and Religious Vegetarians (SERV).[31] Members of the following faiths can find helpful information on this site: Baha'i, Buddhism, Christianity, Hinduism, Islam, Jainism, Judaism and Judeo/Christian, Paganism and Native Religions. In some cases the religious citations appeal to the health benefits of a plant-based diet. In many cases, compassionate treatment of animals is called for in a manner that is incompatible with current nutrition habits of much of the world's population.

Since the proposed approach to investing consists of deviating from a generic index-based formula, it should be comforting to all vegan investors that faith-based investors tend to add to the demand for companies that rank higher on social metrics. The prices of stocks are largely determined by supply and demand, so it is helpful to own shares of a company whose stock is on an upward track in appeal rather than the converse. Specifically, if a given company stock is being purchased by indifferent index investors, faith-motivated investors and vegans, this sustains the collective demand for its shares. Conversely, if there are large classes of investors shunning stocks of a specific company or sector (e.g., fossil fuels), this negative momentum also contributes to a vegan investment approach.

Loan Funds

In a number of faiths, there are opportunities to loan money to various funds connected to the needs of the mission. In some cases, as mentioned earlier (e.g., conservancy organizations), this can be a win-win. There are some notable instances of church debt defaults, so this is an area that requires close scrutiny. A review with an independent advisor not associated with the faith-based organization is highly recommended.

Some faiths have well-established financial service providers. When this is the case, establishing an account requires no more effort than opening a new bank account. Otherwise, such an arrangement may only be worthwhile when a significant amount of money is involved. Interest rates will vary depending upon the term of the debt and circumstances that can go beyond normal market forces (e.g., supply and demand, risk of principal loss). Interest rates that are lower than comparable secular fixed-income investment options can be attractive to an investor with a motivation to support the institutions of their faith. It is not unusual to see very attractive interest rates in some circumstances. In some cases, faith-based borrowers pass along some of the savings they achieve by not having to access loans with relatively higher rates from traditional banking institutions. Unfortunately, in other cases the rates are high to reflect the potential risk for default and/or the use of poor risk-management practices.

Charitable Gift Annuity (CGA)

As an alternative to an outright gift, a charitable gift annuity may be appropriate. Since most of us do not know how long we are likely to live, the use of immediate fixed annuities are sometimes used to cover "longevity risk". For individuals who wish to make an irrevocable gift to their faith during their lifetimes, a CGA can provide lifetime supplemental income, a portion of which will be tax exempt. This option is subject to minimum age requirements and should only be used when all of the implications are evaluated (e.g. impact of inflation, loss of estate value, benefits of laddering gifts over a time in order to meet the desired objective). Due to factors that may be unique to your circumstances, it is very appropriate to consult a financial advisor who is acting in

Chapter 13

Just Deserts

My hope is that I have identified a collection of investment ideas in reasonable alignment with a vegan worldview. Furthermore, by identifying a low fee solution, I aspire to make this specific example of impact investing accessible to a broader audience.

The rewards of moving beyond the more prevalent investment styles, such as passive-index investing, may provide the personal satisfaction of:

- not supporting or profiting from industrial activity that is in clear conflict with your worldview,
- being part of a collective effort to advance a vegan worldview by incrementally raising the social value of companies that you invest in,
- potentially obtaining some relative financial benefit, should your worldview become realized over the course of your investment time horizon,
- increasing awareness of the societal benefits of vegan values (e.g. human, animal and planetary health).

I believe that broader use of vegan investing can take veganism to a higher, more active, level. The use of investment dollars can only amplify the vegan voice in a way that maintains clarity. The act of "putting your money where your mouth is" lends credence to an earnest striving to live one's values.

Given the lack of widely accepted ratings of corporate citizens from a vegan worldview, the concept of low fee vegan investing is, admittedly, in its infancy. Also, there may be a lack of a sufficient number of investment advisors who are in a position to assist vegans, should interest accelerate at too rapid a pace. Patience may be needed. Should significant demand materialize and persist, however, I could certainly see the day when vegan mutual funds and exchange traded funds will be available. If and when a vegan worldview is more objectively articulated, the possibility of a low cost vegan index fund may become realized as well.

The history of sustainable investing over the past several decades has illustrated that investor activism and selectivity can influence corporate behavior for the better. This yields slow, yet steady, benefits to society at large. The greater participation of vegan investors in this area presents a significant opportunity to accelerate these benefits.

Bibliography

1) *Low Fee Socially Responsible Investing* by Tom Nowak, CreateSpace, 2012.
2) *The China Study* by T.Colin Campbell, PhD, and Thomas M. Campbell II, BenBella Books, 2006.
3) https://www.motifinvesting.com/. Accessed 8/8/2014. Brokerage fees noted were current at the time of publishing and are subject to change.
4) https://www.folioinvesting.com/. Accessed 8/8/2014. Brokerage fees noted were current at the time of publishing and are subject to change.
5) http://www.pbs.org/newshour/bb/business-july-dec08-crisishearing_10-23/. Accessed 8/8/2014.
6) http://www.stockpickr.com/pro/portfolio/Warren-Buffett/. Accessed 8/8/2014
7) *Keynes's Way to Wealth* by John F. Wasik, McGraw-Hill Education, 2014, page 46.
8) The Essential Buffet, Timeless Principles for the New Economy, by Robert G. Hagstrom, John Wiley & Sons, Inc., 2001, page 163
9) http://en.wikipedia.org/wiki/Peter_Lynch. Accessed 8/8/2014.

10) *Whole* by T. Colin Campbell, Phd with Howard Jacobson, PhD, BenBella Books, 2013.

11) *The Starch Solution*, by John A. McDougall and Mary McDougall, St Martins Press, 2012.

12) *Prevent and Reverse Heart Disease: The Revolutionary, Scientifically Proven, Nutrition-Based Cure* by Caldwell B. Esselstyn Jr.M.D., Penguin Group, 2007.

13) *Food Choice and Sustainability, Why Buying Local, Eating Less Meat, and Taking Baby Steps Won't Work* by Dr. Richard Oppenlander, Langdon Street Press, 2013, pages 15,77,90 and 93,respectively.

14) *This is Hope, Green Vegans and the New Human Ecology* by Will Anderson, Earth Books, 2012, page 37.

15) http://www.greenvegans.org.   Accessed 8/10/2014

16) http://www.cdc.gov/tobacco/data_statistics/fact_sheets/fast_facts/. Accessed 8/8/2014

17) http://citizensclimatelobby.org/   Accessed 8/8/2014.

18) http://gofossilfree.org/ Accessed 8/8/2014.

19) *The Power of Passive Investing, More Wealth with Less Work*, by Richard A. Ferri, John Wiley & Sons, Inc., 2011.

20) http://www.ipcc.ch/. Accessed 8/9/2014

21) htttp://www.carbontracker.org/site/wastedcapi
tal. Accessed 8/9/2014

22) http://iroquoisvalleyfarms.com/ Accessed
8/9/2014.

23) www.FarmlandLP.com. Accessed 8/9/2014.

24) http://en.wikipedia.org/wiki/Vegetarianism_b
y_country Accessed 8/9/14.

25) http://citizensclimatelobby.org/wp-
content/uploads/2014/06/REMI-carbon-tax-
report-62141.pdf Accessed 8/9/14.

26) http://ussif.org Accessed 11/25/2014.

27) http://en.wikipedia.org/wiki/List_of_S%26P_
500_companies#Recent_changes_to_the_list_
of_S.26P_500_Components. Accessed
8/9/2014.

28) http://www.greenamerica.org/. Accessed
8/10/2014.

29) The Essential Buffet, Timeless Principles for
the New Economy, by Robert G. Hagstrom,
John Wiley & Sons, Inc., 2001, page 127.

30) The Bogleheads' Guide to Investing, by
Taylor Larimore, Mel Lindauer and Michael
LeBoeuf, John Wiley Sons, Inc., 2006, page
109.

31) http://www.serv-online.org/index.htm.
Accessed 8/10/2014.

ABOUT THE AUTHOR

Tom Nowak, CFP®, is founder and Principal of Quantum Financial Planning LLC, an hourly, fee-only financial planning and Registered Investment Advisory firm located near Grayslake, Illinois. He is a member of The Garrett Planning Network, Inc., a nationwide network of professional fee-only financial advisors. Founded by Sheryl Garrett, CFP®, members of the Garrett Planning Network share a common goal – to make competent and objective advice accessible through hourly, as-needed financial planning. Tom is also a member of the National Association of Personal Financial Advisors (NAPFA), the largest professional association of comprehensive, fee-only financial planners in the United States. He is a member of The Forum for Sustainable and Responsible Investment (US SIF). His first book, *Low Fee Socially Responsible Investing, Investing in your worldview on your terms*, was published in March of 2012. He may be reached at: info@quantumfinancialplanning.com.